Praise fɔ_  s
on Customer Experience

"Nick Glimsdahl's detailed and meaty masterpiece, *Reasons NOT to Focus on Customer Experience,* gives clear direction on how to take the business to the top of the charts."
— JIM KNIGHT, CX Speaker, Author, Podcaster, CEO bookstarPR

"With a flair for the dramatic, this book gets right to the point."
— DAN GINGISS, author of *The Experience Maker*

"Nick gets his point across very clearly using this resource."
— NATE BROWN, Co-Founder of CX Accelerator

"Finally, the comprehensive list you've been waiting for is here."
— NICK ZEISLER, author of *We're Doing CX Wrong...And How to Get It Right*

"Don't judge a book by its cover – this book is focused on taking action."
— BILL STAIKOS, Senior Vice President, Industry Solutions at Medallia

REASONS <u>NOT</u> TO FOCUS ON CUSTOMER EXPERIENCE

- A Comprehensive Guide -

NICK GLIMSDAHL

To book an event or for information about special discounts for bulk book purchases, please contact Nick Glimsdahl at nicholas@glimsdahl.com, or visit www.press1fornick.com.

Manufactured in the United States of America.

To my bride, Michelle, and the A-Team.

Contents

Prologue

Most of this book will be <u>blank</u> because there are no legitimate reasons NOT to focus on the customer experience.

Each chapter will start with a list of questions you can use as conversation starters.

I invite you to use this resource not only to provoke thought, but also as a functional notebook. And I'd love to hear from you about the conversations and reactions this book ignites. Please reach out to me via press1fornick.com or email me at nicholas@glimsdahl.com.

Chapter 1

Customer Experience

"You've got to start with the customer experience and work back toward the technology – not the other way around."
—Steve Jobs

Questions

- What is Customer Experience?
- What does it mean to you?
- If you have a strong strategy, do you need a CX program?

Chapter 2

Employee Experience

"The way you treat your employees is the way they will treat your customers."
—Sir Richard Branson

Questions
- What is the correlation between Customer Experience (CX) and Employee Experience (EX)?
- Should you start with EX first?
- How does EX impact retention?

Chapter 3

Digital Transformation

"There is no alternative to digital transformation. Visionary companies will carve out new strategic options for themselves — those that don't adapt, will fail fast."
—Steve Jobs

Questions

- How will your customers have input in the Digital Transformation?
- How can you prioritize Digital Transformation?
- How do you measure if the transformation was successful?

Chapter 4

Culture

"Corporate culture matters. How management chooses to treat its people impacts everything for better or worse."
—Simon Sinek

Questions
- What is the correlation between culture and CX?
- Should you align the culture with your mission, vision, and values?
- Why should it matter to organization?

Chapter 5

Marketing

"Either write something worth reading or do something worth writing about."
— Benjamin Franklin

Questions
- What role does marketing play in the CX and EX?
- When and how should marketing be involved in CX?
- Should marketing be involved in the customer journey?

Chapter 6

Contact Center

"Customers who are merely satisfied remain your customers only as long as everything goes their way."
— Chip Bell

Questions

- How would a cloud contact center help a company focus on CX and EX?
- Should a business focus on CX, EX, and business outcomes when improving the contact center?
- What should be measured in a contact center to make sure a company focuses on the customer?

Chapter 7

Sales

"How you sell matters. What your process is matters. But how your customers feel when they engage with you matters more."
—Tiffani Bova

Questions

- How should your organization adapt the sales process to customers' needs?
- Should a sales representative be rewarded on customer lifetime value? Why or why not?
- What is the role of sales in CX?

Chapter 8

Customer Success

"The biggest barrier to customer success is CEOs not making it an important part of the culture."
—Nick Mehta

Questions

- When should a Customer Success (CS) team get involved?
- Should Customer Lifetime Value be a metric for Customer Success?
- What length of time should a CS team stay involved?

Chapter 9

Operations

*"Never tell people how to do things.
Tell them what to do and they will
surprise you with their ingenuity."*
— General George S. Patton

Questions
- How should you align Operations
  with Digital Transformation and CX?
- How can operations reduce friction to
  improve EX and CX?
- How should customer data impact
  decisions within Operations?

Chapter 10

Customer Lifetime Value

"Profit in business comes from repeat customers, customers that boast about your product or service, and that bring friends with them."
— W. Edwards Deming

Questions

- What is the importance of Customer Lifetime Value (CLV)?
- Can CLV justify technology investments?
- How can a company prioritize CLV internally?

In summary, there are *no* reasons not to focus on the customer experience.

ABOUT

Nick Glimsdahl is a speaker, podcast host, contact center strategist, and writer. His mission is to bring together customer expectations, employee needs, and business objectives to create a seamless experience.

Today, Nick hosts the *Press 1 For Nick* podcast, and is the Director of Contact Center Solutions at VDS. *Press 1 For Nick* is both educational and engaging, and each episode offers listeners a dynamic blend of insightful stories, best practices, and invaluable lessons. Nick's guests – each with a unique wealth of knowledge – include leaders from a variety of backgrounds and industries.

You can reach Nick by emailing him at nicholas@glimsdahl.com, visiting press1fornick.com, or scanning the QR code below.

RESOURCES

Book Recommendations

All my book recommendations can be found at
https://press1fornick.com/books/

Glossary of Terms

A Glossary of CX Terms can be found at
https://press1fornick.com/glossary-of-cx-terms/